THE OPPOSITE
OF
LETTING
THE MIND
WANDER

THE OPPOSITE
OF
LETTING
THE MIND
WANDER

Selected Poems
And A Few Songs

By
Keith Waldrop

LOST ROADS PUBLISHERS
Number 36   Providence   1990

The poems and songs in this volume have been published in the following books and chapbooks:

A Windmill Near Calvary (University of Michigan Press, 1968)
The Antichrist (Burning Deck, 1970)
Songs from the Decline of the West (Perishable Press, 1970)
My Nodebook for December (Burning Deck, 1971)
Indifference Point (Limestone Press, 1973)
The Garden of Effort (Burning Deck, 1975)
Three Tenors, One Vehicle (with James Camp and X.J. Kennedy, Open Places, 1975)
Three Logical Poems (Turkey Press, 1975)
Poem from Memory (Treacle Press, 1975)
Windfall Losses (Pourboire Press, 1977)
The Space of Half an Hour (Burning Deck, 1983)
The Ruins of Providence (Copper Beech, 1983)
A Ceremony Somewhere Else (Awede, 1984)
Water Marks (Underwhich Editions, 1987)
Shipwreck in Haven (Awede, 1989)

Library of Congress Cataloging in Publication Data

Library of Congress

Waldrop, Keith
    The opposite of letting the mind wander: selected poems
        and a few songs   /   by Keith Waldrop
    ISBN 0-918786-41-X: $8.95
I. Title.
PS3573.A423067   1989
811'.54—dc20   89-12623
                                cip

Copyright ©1990 by Keith Waldrop; All rights reserved
Published by Lost Roads Publishers
PO Box 5848 Providence RI 02903
First printing by McNaughton and Gunn
Typeset by The Writer's Center, Bethesda MD
Book design by C.D. Wright and Forrest Gander
Cover design by Laynie Browne, Melanie Plowman
Cover art, Small High Valley series numbers 24, 5, 13, by Marjorie Welish

Funded in part by a grant from the Rhode Island State Council on the Arts and by an anonymous donor to the Rhode Island Foundation.

for Brita Bergland

CONTENTS

THE OPPOSITE OF LETTING THE MIND WANDER

Selected Poems And A Few Songs

NOTES FOR A PREFACE

I find it impossible to write—as to read—one thing at a time. The earlier poems of *A Windmill Near Calvary* came while I was finishing a doctoral dissertation; the rather abstract *Garden of Effort* is contemporary with—was balanced by—texts for songs. It's rare that I don't have a litter of fragments and false starts suggesting, often, irreconcilable projects. This does not mean I write fast, only that my concentration is poor.

But one has to work with what one has. Or, if possible, find some way of putting one's defects to work. Inattention can be useful. There is a certain frame of mind—I almost said level of consciousness—which is only open to the easily distracted, the rarely engrossed, a frame of mind that lets in strays and itself tends to digress.

I thought (and think) of it as a problem, not in assimilation (there is always a plenty) but in accommodation—a formal problem. The raw material of this book, to my great surprise as I look at it now, is thoroughly autobiographical, no doubt because my life is what I know best—know even without thinking about it—and am least concerned with. It is there, a convenient support for whatever constructions I can come up with. They are, of course, constructions.

And what fascinates me, in any case, is *background*—those aspects of the scene we can't really scrutinize, cannot (by definition) attend to. They do not survive a spotlight; foregrounding destroys them, simply by picking them out.

*   *   *   *   *

I have excluded here a large percentage of my published poetry, not to disown it, but hoping to provide in this sample a context for the whole. The arrangement is roughly chronological, but very roughly. Publication dates of the individual volumes are quite misleading: *Windfall Losses*, for example, was finished in 1970 and *The Garden of Effort* written in 1971 (except for one earlier section), but these came out in 1977 and 1975 respectively.

The poems—twenty-five years' worth—certainly point different directions, but almost never in distinct periods. Those of *A Windmill Near Calvary* move towards a conversational tone, a movement completed in *Windfall Losses* and picked up again, much later, in *The Ruins of Providence.*

On the other hand, the series of abridgements called *The Antichrist* ("Introducing a Madman," for instance, is the text of *Dracula* with most of the words removed), is only an early example of my preoccupation with collage—my great delight, collage, which one way or another I'm always coming back to.

*   *   *   *   *

My mother, for my own good, plied me with dying words of exemplary individuals, sinners and saints. I came to love the genre (Wyndham Lewis's blast, for instance—someone my mother didn't know about—to a nurse asking about his bowels: "Mind your own business!") and sometimes I think it suggests the ideal poem: not good or bad, but final; not determined by what it says—or even how it says it—but by the blank which follows.

I've accomplished, obviously, nothing so extreme. These poems are tentatives, efforts at pulling together the objects of my wandering attention, at giving shifting and disparate items a place to stand—still temporary, of course, but enduring compared to their life in my head.

from *A WINDMILL NEAR CALVARY*

ANGEL TO LOVE, MAN TO WORLD

I was reared among prophets, who saw
one true Word in a deceiving world and
fixed their gaze on it. I remember (dimly)
stunning silences, and messages—come down
whole from above—and mysteries, in a matrix
like gnashing of teeth.

Now what possesses me? Someone who didn't
know me might take me for a connoisseur—
I stare till I wonder those canvases (for
instance) are not consumed, and expect any day
to see it posted: *défense de manger
les objets d'art.*

It's simple voracity, the garden-of-Eden
chomp. (We see—by and large—what
we want to see. At least that explains
why just looking around us makes us
guilty—by breathing open Adam's eyelid God
damned the mud.)

A shamed child would like, as Erikson
puts it, "to destroy the eyes of the world."
Failing that, he closes his own eyes, tightly.
As for me, I cultivate my field of nothingness
a bit extravagantly. (I know the world exists.
I do not know

how the world exists. I do not know how
I know the world exists. Empty mind
is a greedy darkness. Brightness is
all there is. From a bright point
light pulsates, throb after throb, into the
ravening dark.)

If my retinal sensitivity were increased, I
would perceive, I'm told, not more occult
hills or finer prospects, but irregularities
of the light itself. Strange as it
seems, there's nothing more to see.
(Fabulous world.)

No one thing will do—more and more, nothing
will substitute for anything else. Wrapped
in the accidents of an untasted
apple, even Good and Evil might be appetizing.
And couldn't I regard my death as Eve did hers—
salivating?

I'd like an inclusive mind, where nothing could
possibly be out of the question. Like Saint
Mark's facade where, half way up a
clutter of Christianity and Venetian lace, are
four Roman horses, poised, in place.
Surely it was

thinking like this made Brueghel paint
a windmill near Calvary. When Adam, as it
fell out, got too old to know Eve, he sat
his inspired carcase down by his hoe, watching
his sweaty children screw up generation
after generation.

ANTIQUARY

Some people try, before cashing in, to make
their lives into shrines. Mine seems to be turning out,
as predicted, a small provincial museum, the kind
that might have in some corner or other one work
you could be interested in, if you knew it was there.
Memorials and keepsakes hang around, half catalogued. Some
curiosa, here and there a whopper—who else
could maintain a scarlet nose drinking
Dr. Pepper? I have my precedents. Lots of men
shuffle off, leaving a ball of tinfoil too large to get
out of the attic or half a century of the New York Times
or some other mess. I keep everything. Old
gods and old ads fade together; both
show better on a neutral wall. Philosophies, old hat,
catch dust on a rack. The trouble is
I'm a glutton. The floor is cluttered,
the shelves go across the windows. I trip
sometimes over ancient arguments or
a lid I can't place, or claim two different heads
to be Saint Thomas's. Nothing, nothing will I
surrender. There is little enough as it is.
I may, of course, croak tomorrow, stumbling
from the larder, but I will not set
my house in order.

CONVERSION

I am already sweeping towards my most
permanent state. Keith means "wind," according
to *What to Name the Baby*. There is
a paradise promised for those who despise
whatever turns—flesh going sour—and I
have despised it.

But I have been converted. Stock dreams can be
flicked on, the assured voice forming first and
then, slowly, its radiant body, but they fulfill
no wish of mine. All my aerier hopes
have dwindled to a momentary point of light,
disappearing.

Reality is what does not change, i.e., reality
is what does not exist, held desperately.
All my past sins I attribute to a
commerce with angels, someone else's. The
earth brings forth of itself and the rest is only
worth a thought.

Now faces crop out of the most random
inorganic patterns, usually nobody's in particular
—I take them as a less specific, less
beautiful, Allegory of Spring. Sometimes,
at night, my head swerves in a rising spiral
of labyrinthine

vertigo, descending only in the arc of sleep.
But I have learned to like the dust I am fed by
winds that shift across an actual world.
I am already what I will be later. And the cycles
shorten. I owe letters to so many, I doubt
that I will ever catch up now.

CREDO

It is a great doctrine that says we
believe as much as we deserve. Saint Thomas was worth,
apparently, everything in the *Summa*, though he couldn't stomach
the Immaculate Conception. Mrs. Katache of Arkhangelsk
supposes she's a chamber pot and shrieks to be emptied.
What does one have to do, or be, to accept
streets of gold or the big lift at the Rapture? Perhaps
Gregory, for his compassion, was allowed to imagine sinners
scorching out their stains in Purgatory.
I know a Christian, says she
just has to laugh thinking of all those atheists going to
wake up in Hell. There are those for whom God is
dead, but who fear the Devil or my black cat. I think
the time is coming and maybe now is when the tree that
overshadows this house will grow from my forehead, spreading
like veins, ring after ring.

HORROR STORY

I had two
grandfathers. One was a bald gentle postmaster
in Leeton, Missouri; he died and was buried.
The other was some kind of preacher;
I never saw him. The terrible thing about
ghosts is that we know they are not there.
Two grandmothers. One chased me with a
broom because I accused her of riding it.
The other stopped listening and went deaf.
They both survived their husbands, but
now they are both dead. My father is
dead too, but this is no elegy.
I was disappointed early, by lack of precision.
I found it hard to keep a grip
on outlines. They always slip.
The fine delineation swells
around the edges, where it smells.
Woman, be strange, take me with your eyelid.
Nothing in dead landscapes suggests terror.
I have married a wife whose
surface I adore. And other surfaces.
Who knows what may leap out from the shadows?
Loved houses are haunted. And I have
no explanation.

LUNCH

The table is loaded. I marvel at my
appetite. I wonder if the void I stuff
is symbolic. At sixteen I considered
suicide and decided against it, on
purely hedonistic grounds. In his last days
my father got overweight, living alone, on
lima beans and schnapps. My brother Julian was
reduced at Leavenworth but now he lets his belly
hang out of his shirt as he feeds steaks to his
cat and laughs at the bulging globe. The Marquis de Sade, too,
eventually ate himself obese, while training lunatics
to act out in public his very personal complexes.
I marvel at all great appetites: Doctor Johnson,
Thomas Aquinas, Wolgamot. Food is Brahman, the text says,
and I suppose the devil, then, is the stuff
I void. People have eaten themselves to death,
and now, here, at this loaded table, it's hard to remember
how for a long time they had to coax and even force me
to open my mouth to the few things I disliked less
than the rest; it is hard now to imagine
such connoisseurship.

from *THE ANTICHRIST*

THE CENTURIES

(an abridgement of Tolstoy's *War and Peace*)

A strange lady, the one
who had been talking to the priests,
rose and offered him
her seat. It was not the question
"What for?" but the question "How?"
that interested him.

"I have had a proposition made me
concerning you,"
he said with an unnatural
smile. And the count turned
to the cook, who with a shrewd and respectful expression
looked observantly and
sympathetically at the father and son.

He had a dim perception of the
following budget.

"For God's sake, I
implore you, come at
once, if
you do not wish to make me and
the whole family wretched,"
wrote the countess.

"I suppose it has to be like this," she thought.

Two doors led from the room,
one straight
on into what had been the
drawing . . . "Well?" asked Napoleon. "The chessmen
are set up, the game
will begin tomorrow!" It was
hot.

He seated
himself more
comfortably, and
coughed, evidently
preparing to tell a long story.

He was armed with a
musketoon (which he
carried rather as
a joke), a pike and an
axe. She blushed, pressed her clasped
hands on her
knees, and then,
controlling herself with an evident
effort, lifted
her head
and began to speak rapidly.

Paper money may deceive the ignorant,
but nobody is deceived
by tokens of base
metal that have no
value but merely
jingle.

DEGENERATION

He is conceited about a disease
memory makes possible.
Immeasurable vistas down the dusk
made him adherent of a vague socialism,
indistinct, faulty, obscure. The singer
proposes to go to a modest restaurant;
he does not understand his natural impulses.
No completely sound mind—vague, barren,
fraternal—feels its vital internal
processes. In higher organisms
all progress rests on this: he
does not allow the imagination the prospect
of being thrashed or kicked.
For Kant, in the small town of Königsberg,
like every other complex and highly
developed human being, has not the remotest
connection. When he makes them
speak, he must first
translate.
The capacity for attention has diminished.

INTRODUCING A MADMAN

He finished his speech in a
gruesome way. Ha! Ha!

I can feel it wet round
her neck, for now
both mother and daughter lay in it, more
radiantly beautiful than ever.

Introducing a madman: My God!
what has happened to him?

Crush me with fear and
horror, you so
clever lady (with a
strength which seemed incredible).

from *WINDFALL LOSSES*

COMMUNICATION

No sooner is the tea into my teacup
and Rosmarie settled comfortably, across
the room, into Proust's world, I
begin this scratching around after some
semblance of elegance.

Does that mean I want
to say something?
I don't think so.

But I confess a hankering after
periodic sentences. Even
while writing some other kind.

As for Earl Grey, whoever
he was, we may assume he preferred
a rough but aromatic brew.

There's an elegant poem by
Swift, on a bride who, unwisely, on her
wedding night, has twelve cups of tea.

The kind of tea not specified.

In experiments by Delgado and
others, miniature electrodes
are implanted in the tissues of the living
brain, and precise charges administered
by radio control. Sham-rage, sham-
sex, sham-sleep are all
available by command.

Charlus's love-life, with such
a device, could have been straightened out.
Maybe also Proust's, and his asthma.

Everyone must have noticed—so
it's nothing much to be saying—how everything
we drink turns to urine. Everything
flows, sooner or later, and the rivers
being, as they are, full of putrid
matter and poison and whatever we've
eliminated, I suggest thinking
twice before stepping in.

Otherwise, for the moment, no
message.

MONEY

Money
is pure spirit. It's what you convert
things into so as to carry their
value without their weight.

Things, everybody agrees, are
interchangeable. Everything
has its price.

Money is the philosophers'
stone.

In the mind, too, the hard
law holds—everything
must be paid for.

You'd think at some point or
other there'd be an unexpected surplus. One of those
chain letters could
come through with four thousand ninety-six
one dollar bills. You can't deny, some
people do seem to make fortunes from
next to nothing.

I treasure Blake's proverb about
the fountain overflowing and, even more, an old
phrase about "a fountain
of gardens." But I'm jotting down here, just so
I won't forget, how feelings that
seem timeless pass
quickly out of currency.

Those who think God created heaven
and earth must consider him
Number One Spendthrift. They must
found their hopes on possible
blunders in his accounting.

It's hell to be poor.

MOTION DISCOMFORT

El Cheapo in the jaws of Camp
pollutes the pressurized air as we
streak in the general direction
of the Houses of Parliament.

And I am thinking over, in my
vague way, some of the possible relations
between this body, those clouds, that
ocean down there.

I'm a bit uncomfortable, but not
really scared. Nothing, in a realm so
purely conjectural, can actually hurt.

I remember a friend, now, who had always taken
for granted that the toilets on airplanes
were just like train toilets, which open onto
the ties beneath.

I think also how Epicurus taught that
all things, being heavy, fall forever, but
gently, without impact, having no
place to land.

for Ihab Hassan

MY NODEBOOK FOR DECEMBER

1

Closing the door is supposed to open some
inward source—as with, for example, the prayer-
closet: the text says go in and "shut thy door."
It's a stroke of luck when traditional
wisdom so matches the turning of the season.

2

I've often thought of writing a poem of grotesque
length (an epic, yes) and setting the entire argument
the instant after Gautama's enlightenment, while
it seemed to him he would pass directly
into Nirvana, while the powers of good trembled
thinking man was lost. It was only an
instant, because of course the Buddha
reconsidered.

3

Bulls for the bull-fight must (this is
absolutely essential) be
innocent. The very brightest are certainly,
by human standards, stupid, but
after a few fights the
dullest among them would learn not to
charge an empty cape but turn and
massacre the fancy-pants who dances there
for a bloody crowd. But, as Hemingway
noted, the bull never survives. I can't, myself, get
excited about "life and death, i.e., violent

death," and have never been able to
work up much sympathy for
the brute who runs with his
head down *or* for the show-off, who
has it coming. I'll probably never
develop a taste for battle or
get seven novels written or kill myself.

4

History is hard for me. I've no
sense for it.

5

The world—and if ever there was a self-evident
proposition, here it is—the world
is a big fish. I've caught it in
my net. And now, long into the winter
nights, wearily, I study my net.
The fish stinks.

6

A friend talks passionately in favor of
silence. I listen to him. He says, "Silence
dissolves the categories" and "Silence renews
the potential of consciousness." And it strikes me
that I should say something.
But I've never been able to argue. And whenever there's
been a choice between speaking and keeping still,
I've kept my mouth shut. Well,
usually. And only after
a certain amount of prodding I've
produced the necessary conventional sounds,
feeling the thread of words I spew
inordinately fragile, certainly nothing
to depend on. Whereas the craw of
silence is vast and, anyway,

already has us—it's the scorching sunlight
of a Nilescape or the wind across the Great
Plains, burying us. Friend, waist deep in dust or
sand, maybe we'd contrive a gesture.

7

I passed the peak of my
energy at the age of—it's
hard to believe—
twelve. Since then,
little by little, I've collected
the furniture of my house.
I teach meanwhile, and I
study, but no one knows
my specialty.

8

XMAS (after Pessoa)

A God is born. Other Gods die. Truth
has neither come nor gone, only the Error has changed.
We have now another Eternity,
and the world is no better off than it was.
Blind Science plows a sterile plain.
Lunatic Faith lives a dream of worship.
A new God is nothing but a word.
Seek not. Nor believe. All is occult.

9

Time is molecular—so much for
Zeno—and each moment brings everything
out of nothing. In the beginning (each
beginning) the universe is only a
point—no dimension—and then
it's a world, for a moment, and
each moment is apocalypse. *Continuous
creation* it used to be called, and now
we say *expanding* universe, because (I
forgot to say) each moment is more. Whatever else it may
be it's always more. No wonder the poet cries
"Oh, Oh,"
or, on a higher level, lyrical verses. But don't
worry. I'm not violent. We all
live in a residue of
bright pulsations, a gob
of time, an after-image.

10

How naive can you get?—I
was wondering, when the Great
Year comes around to this point again
and the next me sits signing his
poems Keith Waldrop, will he
remember back across the void
of Decembers to where I drift into these
speculations? And a moment's
thought answers my stupid question: I
remember nothing.

11

When I think of the books you could
fill with what I don't know, *oof.* The pressing need's
for a phenomenology of ignorance. Everything has
horizons, and they're not just
out of sight, they loom. Yes, and they beckon.
An open door is plain and simple, like a
wall. A closed door is an invitation. But if
the knob is turning . . . ?
Well, I'm closing in, or opening up. I've been so
bloody finicky the mysteries catch me sometimes
with my lids down. But I'm preparing. I need
many voices for my revenge.

TO ROSMARIE IN BAD KISSINGEN

I just squashed a fat
fly who was buzzing me, but he's
more disgusting dead.

If we go by numbers, my old
zoology prof used to say, this
is the age of insects,
more specifically: of beetles.

This is also the age of information.

I hope the churchbells
of Bad Kissingen aren't
keeping you awake—though it's
nice, hearing tones decay. You
won't let the bells chase you to church.

Somebody, just the other day, claimed
that you and I haven't
any roots (he thinks that's bad). It's
true enough that we've fallen between
two generations—one drunk, the other
stoned. The one has
inhibitions to get rid of (you know
what that means: liquor and
analysis); the other, a great
blank space to fill.

The wars of the young I
think will be wars of religion.

But all this letter is really
meant to say is that you should
leave those Kraut Quasimodos at their
glockenspiels and
hurry back here, because whatever we
don't see together has for me always
a dead spot somewhere,

even though I know that one
place is much the same as another,

and all the air we could
breathe anywhere in the world
has already, numberless times, been the
breath of a fern and
a marigold
and an oak.

from *THE GARDEN OF EFFORT*

A HATFUL OF FLOOD

1

Outside the calendar,
werewolves and other
danger spots.

• ● •

Almost everybody, you
know, is dead.

• ● •

Teeth, nails and
hair—what a moving
landscape.

• ● •

Two segments of
horizon, haggling
over a birthday.

2

Am I a prisoner?

• ● •

Pumpkins, by
gouging, given
eyes, nose, grin.

• ● •

Remember me only
by what I've
said in my sleep.

• ● •

Corridors and boxes, swell
of little cells.

• ● •

Empty? Filled?

• ● •

Time. The fatness
of time.

3

A face at the
window and I forget
I'm indoors.

• ● •

Their language, in
so many senses.

• ● •

I, a region
of you, a
region of me.

• ● •

Our system un-
stable—evidence
in time.

• ● •

Enormous eyes of
Christians or
decadent pagans.

• ● •

Some things I've
seen through and
vice versa.

• ● •

Worth everything
but not necessarily
worth while.

• ● •

In different
groupings, an
instant, as if it
were an instant.

• ● •

Not bodies, but
"entities
carefully abstracted."

• ● •

The unlived life is
not worth examining.

4

What happens
at the exact
center?

• ● •

Consciousness
merely the
environment.

• ● •

Pianos, complex
as they are, not
to be considered
our rivals.

• ● •

I remember
everything and it's
all wrong.

• ● •

Jump ahead and
no one is alive.

• ● •

Convergence
to a web:
nearer, farther.

• ● •

Nearer.

5

Bonelike light, straining
in patterns
of a dozen arbitrary
figures.

• ● •

Half expected.

• ● •

Fading—I'm
dredging, between
dreams.

• ● •

The obscurer
euphemisms. Gossip
of kindergartens.

• ● •

My proper
doorstep, and a
shadow, face down.

6

Absence as
object of fetish.

• ● •

History recuperating.

• ● •

Sick with
reminiscence, unless
I remember.

• ● •

Discovering a
dead end. Go on
and conjecture.

• ● •

The vague
concept of
arrival.

• ● •

In broad
daylight, there were
no more symptoms.

7

Joy and pain
rejoice the
soul, being
physical.

• ● •

The better games the
hard ones.

• ● •

A sense of
tricycling
through the void.

• ● •

Or, at least, a
chance of losing.

• ● •

And, well yes, even
if broken,
rules.

8

What carol, what margin
of error can compare
with the history of France?

• ● •

From one corner of
the hall even
to the other.

• ● •

The earth—such
suspense.

• ● •

Various more or less
recondite linguistic
problems or tea.

9

Your body poses
no problem.

• ● •

Still on the surface.

• ● •

This an
occasion of lucidity.

• ● •

You reflect. You
scatter.

• ● •

Flowing
light, your outline.

• ● •

It takes a
moment to
see you.

• ● •

The sunniest embrace
radiates vagueness.

• ● •

Elementary spectre.

• ● •

Play, our
symmetries.

• ● •

Otherwise
clear, dark.

10

Starting
from 'here.'

• ● •

A look in all
directions, not—to be
sure—at once.

• ● •

The garden of effort.

• ● •

The damned
cannot say
'now.'

SONGS

AUTOBIOGRAPHY

As I came across the water where
I knew the wrecks lay deep,
It might have scared me silly if
I hadn't been asleep.
It would have scared me silly
If I'd realized how high
The waves were heaving upward towards
The history of the sky.

As I crawled onto the shore where
Factories were going full blast,
The noise would have left me deafened if
I hadn't crawled on past.
And it almost turned my stomach,
Looking up, to see how high
The stacks were belching smoke up towards
The history of the sky.

As I trudged along in the desert where
The sand stretches out forever,
It began to dawn on me that here
It wouldn't help me to be clever.
The sand stretched out forever like
A lake of perfect dry,
and reflected the unmoving of
The history of the sky.

As I look out my window to where
A few nice days have ruined the snow,
The trees stand over their shadows and
The shadows look ready to go.
And the houses sit as if they think
They'll someday learn to fly.
I've never done anything but drift by under
The history of the sky.

CONNECTICUT ELEGY

In the New England winter,
When creeks no longer ran,
I put my garbage outside
In a standard galvanized iron can.

In the New England night,
While snow lay deep,
A skunk tipped my can over
And my garbage man Pippin died in his sleep.

Pippin my garbage man is dead,
His umbrella has fallen shut.
He chews the dandelions by their roots now,
Rotten under Connecticut.

In the New England spring,
When creeks began to run,
The snow thawed in patches,
Exposing my garbage-littered uncut lawn.

In the New England ground,
Where summer prods the shoot,
Dust waits for a great concussion
To hang in clouds on the air, like fruit.

Pippin my garbage man is dead,
His umbrella has fallen shut.
He chews the dandelions by their roots now,
Rotten under Connecticut.

DO NOT DISTURB

If, when you've gotten past the door that's always locked,
Down the corridor they say is there, and if the passage isn't blocked,
And if you find the stockroom where the things we want are stocked,
Wake me then.

Or if you reach a cloudy gate, and if you make it through,
And if you find the treasuries of snow and rain and dew,
And bring back *all* the colors, to replace our few,
Wake me then.

Or if you get across the ocean that's larger than our own,
And reach the fallen angels howling around their fallen throne,
And can tell me about their darkness, darker than I've known,
Wake me then.

Or if you come to a garden where a tree is blazing like ice,
A place in which even the most unique thing happens twice,
And if you're absolutely certain that it's free *and* Paradise,
Wake me then.

Or if, in your adventures, you should stumble on the place
From which all power flows like water pouring from a vase,
And then if, after seeing that, nothing else can ever be the case,
Wake me then.

Or if your plans wreck and go down, but if you keep
Exploring taste by taste the extreme flavors of the deep,
And if you come to rest in some more satisfying spot to sleep,
Wake me then.

FALL SONG

I can't say for sure that I'll always love you.
I've started so many projects and finished so few,
It's less and less often now I open a book and read it through,
But we'll see.

I won't put up any parp about the infinite
Or argue from predestination that we couldn't ever quit,
It wouldn't do to swear we'll never get tired because I have to admit
It could be.

Knives break, comfortable rocking chairs get so they creak,
The air goes out of air-mattresses and canoes begin to leak.
The Sheik gets too old to do it any more—even the Son of the Sheik,
Eventually.

So we'll see, it could be that I'll come to need total rest,
Or walking past a foreign post office find I've forgotten your address,
But on the other hand there's really very little to be said for emptiness,
So yes,
Let's just see.

And if you want to know what I think, remember what I told you.
All these doubts are a bill of goods I wouldn't want to have sold you,
I think I may die not grabbing for life so much as just groaning to hold you
One more season.

PAPER

Somebody told me I wouldn't know how to choose
Between presidential candidates if I didn't read the news,
And wouldn't even know who's out on bail for what crimes,
So I subscribed to the daily and the Sunday *Times*
And all that paper piles up
On the sofa, on the floor,
In the wastebaskets and in front of the door,
On the sills, and I can't see
Out my window anymore.

I went through a magazine and clipped all the book-club come-ons
And they sent very friendly bills and then they threatened to
    send a summons,
And they kept sending me monthly selections, and alternates,
    and when
I wrote them to stop they didn't but they billed me again
And all that paper piles up
On the sofa, on the floor,
In the wastebaskets and in front of the door,
On the sills, and I can't see
Out my window anymore.

The other day I hunted in every corner of every drawer
Our marriage certificate, though I can't remember just what for,
And I found old notebooks and loose sheets and scraps in illegible
    condition
And both our lives scribbled out and wadded in every conceivable
    position.
And all that paper piles up
On the sofa, on the floor,
In the wastebaskets and in front of the door,
On the sills, and I can't see
Out my window anymore.

And while I was digging around, at the back of a bottom shelf
I came across a dog-eared spineless mildewed *Song of Myself,*
So I gave it to a friend and in return for what I'd given
He sent me a complete *Congressional Record* back to eighteen
    forty-seven
And all that paper piles up
On the sofa, on the floor,
In the wastebaskets and in front of the door,
On the sills, and I can't see
Out my window anymore.

Rivers are clogging with *Time, Life, Evergreen,* and other soggy
    wisdom.
Some high official in Washington just misfiled the key to the filing
    system.
I can never find my driver's license among all the credit cards and
    such.
You can die for lack of paper or you can die from too much.
And all that paper piles up
On the sofa, on the floor,
In the wastebaskets and in front of the door,
On the sills, and I can't see
Out my window anymore.

SLEEPING BEAUTY

Inside her slumber, she is fast awake.
It is the world around her that is deep.
Any step she wishes she is free to take,
But inside her vigil, there is another sleep.

Sleeping, she knows still whatever she has known:
A palace-full of endless echoing halls.
Any view she takes now is completely her own,
This sleeping castle with its high castle walls.

The thorn-bush that chokes shut all the doors
Conceals the form of her good fairy.
Moonlight picks out glimmers of distant wars
Across the dark original prairie.

Looking, with closed eyes, for an unremembered moment,
She has a hundred-year-long night to squander.
She's her own calendar. Sleep is her catacomb.
The opposite of letting the mind wander
Is letting the mind go home.

SONG FOR CROSSING A BRIDGE

This song started with Eve, my mother,
Who lived in an orchard at one end of the world.
She was offered an apple but she bit into another,
And, ordered out, these were the words she hurled:

Well, shit, we couldn't hold on to it,
It's out the old conduit,
Down the river,
Into the open sea.

A king once died, sitting on the pot,
Watching in his mind's eye his kingdom grow,
And trying to keep a finger on everything he'd ever got—
The core of the problem is letting it go,

Since, shit, you just can't hold on to it,
It's out the old conduit,
Down the river,
Into the open sea.

There's something nice about living while an age is ending
And another is doing its best to be born.
Neither the old nor the new is worth defending—
The flesh on the fruit is there to be torn

Because, shit, nobody can hold on to it,
It's out the old conduit,
Down the river,
Into the open sea.

THE WIND IS LAUGHING

My love and I sat down to lunch,
And while I was tucking my bib
I heard time's teeth come together crunch
And I felt a sharp pain in my rib.

And I thought how the years get short while days get longer
And how old men get weak, old women stronger,
And the wind I feel now feels nice to me,
But later the same wind will blow right through me,
And the wind is laughing.

My love and I sat down to dinner,
And while I was fanning my soup
My love said my hair was looking thinner
And I felt my shoulders beginning to stoop.

And I thought how although it's likely I'll still adore her
The safest bet is always to bet on horror,
And the wind I feel now feels nice to me,
But later the same wind will blow right through me,
And the wind is laughing.

My love and I got up for breakfast,
And while I was gulping my yolk
My love, whose laugh is quick as the quickest,
Laughed, and we laughed till I thought I would choke.

And I know the air is poison and no waters healing
And years are going to blow by forever without feeling,
But the wind we feel now feels nice to us,
And later the same wind will blow right through us,
But the wind is laughing.

from *A CEREMONY SOMEWHERE ELSE*

ARCHIPELAGO

The wildness of birds, with
regard to man, is a particular
instinct directed against
him. Sailors, wandering
through the wood in
search of tortoises, take
cruel delight
in knocking down the little birds.
Pursued and injured, they learn
a salutary dread.

Only children
"explain." From the ocean
all horrors.
Wanderings, my
home, at
extraordinary
speeds. Carrying on-
wards. "I,"
a vague
term.

The shores of the larger
islands are
fringed with a dense
barrier of mangroves, backed
by impenetrable
thicket. As the ridges are ascended,
taller trees and deep green
bushes are covered
with orchids and trailing
moss. Creepers hang down.

Between
stiffening of
terror which is dry
land and

running
from danger which is
thin air, there are always
the uncertain
waters to be crossed. Closest,
meaning most untrue.

Many foreheads sprang
forth without necks. Arms wandered,
unattached to shoulders.
Eyes strayed about, alone,
wanting eyebrows. Creatures were
created with a face on
either side, cattle with heads of men,
hermaphrodites. At last,
a lovely body with limbs and
bloody thoughts around the heart.

Inward speech, pro-
nounced with
elbow-room. Down,
ungraduated degrees of
down. Gradually the light
at an end, below any notion
of heavenly bodies. No longer
a river with banks, or a
bed in the earth with
lines of water running.

One is astonished at the creative
force displayed on these barren, rocky
islands. The tortoises, when
thirsty, are obliged to travel. Hence
broad and well-beaten paths branch off in
every direction, down to the sea-coast.
The Spaniards, by following them, first

discovered the watering-places. A curious
spectacle, these huge creatures traveling onwards with out-
stretched necks, another set returning, having

drunk their fill. Around unknown
qualities, the
flow past,
unaffecting, barely audible, to
painful beyond
message. Instead of mouth,
kiss. "Must come" or "edge,
edge." Every step widens. Only long
ago will there be
no more sea.

HOW TO TELL DISTANCES

Proclus rises from the
surface of the moon, between
fecund and serene
seas, both dry. Long
corridors and unexpected
rooms. One hears
the voice of the page,

aware of bosom. Emphasis
on the simple solids. All our
decorations temporary, dry
panels, friezes.
A side gate promises
unconsidered scenery. We spread
into definitions.

*

You are welcome to this
map, though it does not
begin to chart the necessary
roads to any real event.
What is a cause in
general? All the elements of the
universe, with the single exception

of yourself. Most poems, later
or sooner, go unread. I measure
things by my own
change of place. Intense original
heat gradually
radiating into empty
space. Note Leibniz Mountains.

*

Ghosts of authorities. All
one and all not-one. Mermaids and
dragons, goat-footed Pans, statues
that move without contact. The structure
of the cosmos and the
structure of Greek
logic both distant as

the moon. Some symbols intelligible
only to the gods. A last
something. Let me put this finally
in your hands. Disintegration, if
on all levels at once, is
positive. It's touch and go.
Gifts are brief, unaccountable.

INDIFFERENCE POINT

1

Continuance, mere con-
tinuance. Your
lines
prove binding. You
brush aside
blood-frenzy for an
idea like
"tomorrow night."

2

Figures of common
sense afford
translation from "the
heart's desire" and
"the demands of
feeling" but lack
correspondence. You
level me with here.

3

Love, my
Weltanschauung,
indistinct and
impermanent
impression, hardly
there,
gone.
You intimidate.

4

Counted my
don't-cares,
settled
saddleback. Now
that they
grade off,
how shall I keep
my distance?

5

I repent of
nearly
everything I've ever
done. If you
compel me to be safe, I'll
mourn my images. All
I want to see is
the visible.

6

I'll divert my
ear from you. I can
listen you away, into
mere sounds, acoustical
sensations. I
would attack
the inner chambers to
disinherit you.

7

This is the real
morning, and
not the other. There
is no special value in
your fear. To "avoid
unlucky words" is to
"keep a religious
silence."

8

Joy un-
does you. You
are not, what
I thought, a
language, but
only a rhetoric. It
will destroy you—watch—as
we connive.

THREE LOGICAL POEMS

1. A RATIONAL HORIZON

As I grow older, I
am more and more the victim
of misprints. Which reminds me,
I am hungry. I believe
in evil, but what
good does it do?
Opposites do not attract
me. No madness seems
improbable. I sleep in
utter peace, a willing
rift in the sampling.

Small gaps in
vocabulary strain my
senses. Look here,
the sky is a washout.
I travel through
distances at some
sort of angle. A level of
feeling conceals
**profounder neutralities, hiding
right under our
favorite responses.**

The horizon fails, from so
many obstacles—they
will not allow it to
be sensible. It would cut
through hills and houses, although
remaining local. The soul's
exile and its highest
interest both register
famine. I
circle, assuming the universe
to be an individual.

2. COOKBOOK ILLUSTRATIONS

The food in these
pictures might goose an
appetite without
answering
any need but
vertigo. It is no more
necessary to eat than
to be hungry. We feel
the fall from any
great height, however
visionary. The abstract curve
takes us, whether
weightless image or heavy
body. Something in the schema un-
nerves us at the edge, suggesting
on over. Old
recipes for ordinary
apple pie began, if one can
trust Betty
Crocker, "First
make your coffin."

3. THE ENDS OF THE EARTH

"This" is
real. What
else? A
harmony determines
the bounds.

The sky, with its
crowds, an
instant. Knowledge
proves
desire.

Let me suppose
a moment.
Fiction
sustains its
intermissions.

Chains to be
investigated, like
purposes. At the
last, tenderly,
a loophole.

All-pervading
staccato. My
intervals,
the elements.
"Now."

THREE POEMS OF POSITION

1. SAILING THE WALL

Now again, trees issue leaves,
obscuring our perspectives. Each
glints its individual green,
leaving a single impression of foliage,

simple but inexhaustible—like
a thousand names for one deity, reflecting
brilliant attributes in qualities of shadow.

Thus obstructed, our possibilities
proliferate. An ambush in suspense.
Gesture too complex to be realized.

Nearing us now, noon
branches downward, into our shelter.
Treasure is only treasure if buried.

Out beyond this region of veins,
the cosmos persists in instant-to-
instant perfection. I like the way
things sound, a sense of previous riverbeds.

2. STANDING

At the end of long marches, food appears
as hunger. Strict separation of sight and
bite characterizes the "God-like erect."

On this field, where there are
no new lessons, we stand small
chance: fury against fervor, principles vs.
principles, legion opposed to legion.

In getting up, we create a commonwealth,
establish the necessary conditions for
slapstick. We are ready to walk.

I have no faith in what this will
say or not say. In campaign after
campaign, the legs support the body
like columns.

"Poor fellows! Poor fellows!" Smoke rising
crosses falling night. We will not
meet, after today's losses.

3. A DELICATE EMPIRICISM

Under the threshold, unconscious
residues support my coming
and my going.

Fantastic moments, like Athens, Sparta,
Thebes, project their landscape
on our empty walls.

The nature of a subject depends on
that of the predicate. Starting with
an indescribable gesture, we
maneuver towards our farthest east.

By now the example with which I
began begins to lose its rank as
paradigm. I could have begun

with any other instance and still
arrive at the same doorway, where
this cat is on that mat.

from *THE SPACE OF HALF AN HOUR*

POEM FROM MEMORY

> *"A lost notion, then, which we*
> *have entirely forgotten, we cannot*
> *even search for."*
>
> —*Saint Augustine*

If one
smokes, there
is the burnt
match, the
butt,
the ashes. There are
crusts, crumbs, spit
out pits. There
is body.
I recall my
body, because it is
present.
And because I
reach out, sifting
ruins for
old manuscripts.
The sense
of the past
springs from
familiarity with
already things. Faces
with nothing new,
stale
objects, received
communications. The
sense of the
present also.
Presentiments appear out of
a dark ground, a
nudge of
sexual fluids. I've
been looking for
you. Everywhere.
In all the obvious
moments, but also
along odd
interfaces. My

father used to
go into
a rage, if anything
was misplaced. Anger
was his order.
It seems fitting we
leave his grave
unmarked, who
always said, when he
could think of
nothing else to say,
"Well, it's
this
world, and
then the fireworks."
Where
are you?
Associations
are not free.
Geographical, we
extend into the
cosmic. But in stepping a few
steps backwards, I'm
in a different
space, precarious.
As when the statue
descends a fourth.
As you
haunt me with
melodies, un-
placeable because somewhat
mis-sung. The year I
was born gave
birth to monsters.
And every year.
It is possible,
even likely, that
there is no center.
Eternity is
simply time
without us. Before
or after. One has

only the choice to
pick
or to dance.
We dream
before birth.
Perhaps you
inhabit
the desire-body. And
while my
grosser faculties
sleep, you
hover above
the sleeper, sleepless.
And
unrepressed. Show
me, in dreams I
won't remember,
the hell prepared for
sins I've forgotten.
This model has
something
to be said for it.
Every
where is ribbed
with feeling, mixed
emotions.
Childhood, when
the teeth are planted,
overgrown with luxuriant
imagery. My
senses remain
local, but reply with
the universal slang.
At the end of
the world, can
I still stretch out my
hand? I
take one skip at a
time, learning
by terror, always
elsewhere. Between thumb and
index finger, primordial
void. Nothing
remains. Why

should you?
Unthinkable
spaces propel us
into time. And always
the doorbell. My
latest recollection
interests
me least of all.
Nothing helps unless
I can deal
it out of order.
My reminiscences
alter, as the
débris of fall
differs from
spring's débris.
Impulses
pass, strewing
dead pathways.
"Oh I just
wonder," says my
mother, "will
the circle be un-
broken." As
if the statement
were its whole
development, you
hide your energy.
A storehouse
could not
contain such over-
lapping. It is
arguable that I
merely reason
from the present back to
some representation,
just as certain
possibles
present themselves
now.
Then the code tells
all, and
is altogether secret.

*   *   *

Meaning should be
understood, like a
missing Buddha
surrounded by appearances.
I think I
hear distant
waves, though not
sure just
what waves at this
distance would sound like.
Continuity
insists I
fail to move. Rhythm is
stifled by time. My dreams
are experimental.
I need disguises.
Cell-destroying thoughts.
Fossil waters.
"Bell turds." A long
enchantment, like offering
tobacco to the sun.
My relation to
the glass of
water on the
table in
this house at such
and such co-ordinates is
one of thirst and
possibility. I live
in ghost states, caressing
imaginary substances. Moments
smear. You
compare with
clouds, tidal
disturbances, rising and
dissolving across
a field. But
not entirely
favorably. To
live longer in
each instant, as certain

birds are
said to do, would
change a constant
pitch
to pulses. The slightest
backward
glance, and things
cave in. What
hope for whispers, when
evening is broadcast?
Everyone
on the warpath. Me
too. Killed, and it was as
if I had
merely stumbled.
My wife, my
wife would not
look at me.
It occurred to
me that I was
dead, and sure
enough, I
spotted my body.
You cannot
imagine how
hungry birds are,
always. *My*
friend, we
have been killed.
For lack of
everything, I
image anything. In the
shadow of
old analogies. Tunnels
nowhere. All notes struck
from a single string
stretched infinitely.
I waver between
map and
territory, time
and eternity. I
count on a
steep forgetting curve,
unlearning by
interference,

by decay. Tracks
fade. Betweens
come clear. It's
cheaper to let
old rails remain,
a network under
later asphalt.
The layers
communicate. Not a
day goes by, but it
insists on being recorded.
Uncalled for, un-
noticed, there
you are still, with
Jericho's leveled
defences, buried
motives, types of arche-
ology. Lacking in
measure, poor
in grace. It isn't
that I know
anything worth
comment. My only
hope is that I'll
know it when
I see it. What could
reduce a man
to traces?

                    *   *   *

I only know where it
is I'm looking
from what I'm
looking at. Objects
thin into
etymologies. I see
by getting about. I
remember by wanting, eyes
in perpetual
movement.
The future is a

long retrospective, watching
a whole
life pass. The law of
accident assumes the
certainty of error.
Current models
stand in a series of
static displays. Someday
I will forget even
my obsessions. All
souvenirs are phony.
In my train of thought, the scenery
extends for miles,
stripped of breath.
Augustine had a friend who
could recite the *Aeneid*
backwards. Perfection
demands images at
strategic intervals, something
steady on which to
map the random. My world
is in disorder. Like-
wise my schedule. I
live within
acceptable
tolerances. At the
intersection of innumerable
fantasies. Irreconcilables
point me to
my orient. Ambiguous
suns. A shower of
elementaries. Venus rising
from the nutrient broth.
Accidents of sensual
logic. Fringes of
interference. That
doorbell. My path
is undeterminable, through
areas that
fail. Vague
reliefs. Fog at the
borders. The frontier
viscous. In a rage at
being named,
the animals tear them-
selves in two. I reconnoitre

96

the universal momentary,
a spirit traveling for
self-improvement.
Free or directed,
I step from one
message to another, at
the boundary between
masks. Death
distracts from various sensible
speculations
on the cocktail
party problem. I think I'm
done with, well for
example, trains and
in an unguarded
moment the
tracks cross
my mind.

*   *   *

Something is always
pulling, little
balloons full of
sentences. By spurning the
world, my
eyes created me. And each
new sight argues
outward, dead against
circumference. Already
keyed for my
coming, a complex
hierarchy cannot
not communicate. My knowing with-
draws, unknowable, amid
widening rings of
devastation. A sphere
of torment. Pain
expanding. My
face, partially
controlled, contains in
its sounds and silences the

real substance.
Long ranges
curve into bodily
changes. Strains
develop I've never heard
of. Buddha may
indulge in a trace of
smile, but
not laugh. Jesus
blubbers. Individual
things are
real enough. It's only
the sum of things
that's false. Balsa
sawdust on a
vibrating membrane shows
where the force
hinges. Any dream at
all produces an
erection. Explanations
beg for questions,
authorize
versions. I
swallow, but it's
more than enough.
There's some priceless
thingamajig
lost, maybe, because I
keep guard, dragoning
ancient treasure, heaping
around me the
symbols of experience. Green
mist. The cold
gray dawn. Fireflies
among city dwellings. Through
the seasons there are
feasts, festivals. At
night, secretions. I carry
always my blest
cloth. One never
knows when. Units of
account cancel stores
of value. Fear of
infancy is a

donation to the adults.
To take by
lips what survives
in kissing. We
deal with extreme, even
violent hunger. The
tendency to re-
turn, a foreign
body, in
the form of
disgust, close
accord, a well-
defined impasse. The stomach
responds continuously.
Every few years somebody
comes up with Noah's ark, on
one or another
god-forsaken mountain, not
always Ararat. Whatever is
moving is
obviously in the now.
How can I be certain these
are only
machines? The more I
reject, the bigger
my alternative becomes. Furniture
in profusion. Baroque
gaze into exploding
crystal.
The dream is
asleep. There are
other layers. I
am playing with
a woman's breasts.
Partial awakening. Sucking
order, but
too dark to
concentrate.
Magic, it
turns out, is
only a mnemonic.
The standing
sleeper, there's a

clear-cut
position. Sensations of
tone require a world-
view to sustain. Memory
breaks down to
memories. Local
divergences. I'm looking for
the last number. The
devil's there
somewhere, back of
temporary surfaces. If I
scratch far enough,
I'm bound to come
down with something. The
doorbell. The doorbell. And also
the phone rings constantly.
Sexual imagination, derived
from the closed eyes.
Where are you? Where
on earth. I see
everything mine
distance, become
environment. My house, my
room, my body, mind,
my inmost self. A universe
in whoosh. "Postponement
of understanding." Farther and
farther the finer
the analysis. But no
center. Only vectors of
rejection, lines
of force. This
reach.
Open.
Secret.

WATER MARKS

*"Philosophy may in no way
interfere with the actual
use of language; it can in
the end only describe it.*

*"For it cannot give it
any foundation either.*

*"It leaves everything
as it is."*

—Wittgenstein

• 1 •

Even if his dream were
actually connected with
the noise of the rain, he will
not accept the *It is
raining* of someone asleep.

• 2 •

It is raining.

• 3 •

Periods of dream, however—
in, for instance, protracted
fatigue—will erupt into
the waking eye.

• 4 •

It takes a horizontal
world to prop
the blueness of the sky. I
cannot lay a foundation, but must
build on one.

• 5 •

Names bother him. Certain
ways of talking turn
his stomach. Until he
sticks them on as labels:
"I am the house
that - - - built."
(Earthquake gardening.)

• 6 •

In the farthest
clearing, misunderstandings
still spring up.

• 7 •

No description
satisfies him. When he
says what happened,
he no longer finds it
characteristic.

• 8 •

Rain is coming
down so as to flood the ill-
drained streets, destroying
ideas of outside. Even
if his dream were actually
connected

• 9 •

Woven, the net, without
really thinking—is
the process
blind? It is all
edge, all surface. If you
want to be
taken in,
go deep. A
random or a systematic mistake
'explains' everything, whereas
all he wants to know lies
spread to the horizon,
unpronounceable.

•   10   •

Water, if quiet, may
reflect clouds, a
battle, elaborate
ruins, the typical flora.

•   11   •

Pieces of a game—king, queen
castle—protect him from
his old enemy: the fascination
of drifting terms.

•   12   •

"Look here, at this – – –"—there
you have the form of a
solid sentence. Note, at the same
time, that everything changes at
each instant. Ah but each
step I take, *however*
uncertainly, gives so much
constancy
to the waves I'm
working my way through. Look, now,
at how the street
glistens under the rain,
and those creases of light in the
sky are like nothing on earth.

•   13   •

Even if his dream

· 14 ·

If I ask, "How
are the arches fallen?" does it not bridge
questions
of blue sky and foundation?—
for at least *this* holiday.

*

· 15 ·

To use words in
such a way that no
frontier closes on them.

· 16 ·

N.B.: there *are* more
insects in America.

· 17 ·

From certain angles, one may see
what the water reflects and
also the bottom of the lake—like
a world and its
memory—but also, in spots,
the surface itself, which
does not seem
to divide anything from
anything, but simply
presents itself as
surface—serene and still,
such a surface as a god might
walk on (it
supports so easily the deepest
hues), such as
might tempt a man to step

• 18 •

And there *are* things of which—for
some reason—it is
difficult to remind oneself.

• 19 •

Shall we, with our
fingers, set about
repairing a torn
spider web? Such expressions
establish a style—a form
of possession.

• 20 •

Don't
go away. This rain
could be for you a
memory, a fiction,
a metaphor, an allusion to
the universal flood—carrying
expectations of Noah's ark
and the invention of
the rainbow. "This" rain stopped
somewhere around • 10 • , and before
extensive revision. In what
sense can I still
speak of *actual*
rain, even if

• 21 •

And who will care about dirty
water, running in
dirty gutters, down some past or spurious
'now'? (Cf. these usages: "*Now*
that Wittgenstein is dead . . . "*Now* that
the poem is coming to
an end . . . " "*Now* logic must
take care of itself

from *THE RUINS OF PROVIDENCE*

AROUND THE BLOCK

I will go for a walk before
bed, a little stroll to settle
the day's upsets. One thing always
follows another, but
discretely—tree after
telephone pole, for instance, or
this series of unlit houses. One moment follows
another,
helplessly, losing its
place instantly to the next. Each frame
fails, leaving behind
an impression of motion.

As for death, at the moment I
think it strangely overrated.

Who now could build
houses like these? who
could afford to? They loom
in the evening of the
East Side, memory-traces
of sometime wealth. Dust
seems forever settling, but
must somehow recirculate.

Once around the block
will do. Porch after porch projects
its columns, seeming one dark and
continuous dwelling. And fear continues,
eternal night shuttering each
source of light. How
remarkable, how remarkably
pleasant, not to be
asleep, still discriminating
dips in the sidewalk, reading
the difference between shadows.

for Heide Ziegler

CHROMATIC STUDY

> " . . . *a modulation has
> occurred which escaped my
> comprehension.*"
>
> *—Schoenberg*

From here to
you is the shortest distance,
warped over silly
surfaces proper
to a modern universe.

Between one action and another,
there is an empty time, un-
fillable. It's easy enough to
throw oneself against
an adequate breakfast or
carry a dreadful secret even
unto death, but
mile after mile of mere
motion stretches between decisions.

"Listening to a concert," he
continues, "I often find myself,
unexpectedly,
in a foreign country."

Themes float up, in
conversation, that I
at some point noted
and sight now as
familiar objects on a new horizon, thus
known but unknown, recognized
as forgotten.

It takes complicated
projections to give us
ordinary area.

I would like to practice simple
bi-location.

In the Sea of Darkness, a
continent sinks, in *terrible con-*
vulsions. With every
expedition, islands
remove, withdrawing always
to remoter
latitudes, just beyond our
last advance.

Immeasurable, the
ocean of harmony, washing
scraps of tune onto
one or another shore, sloshing in
time, *appoggiatura*
across the Dolphin's
Ridge, each ripple
lost in
long resolves, dissonant
concord of surprising
distances, intervals at
extremes. In the midst
of spray, phantom solids.

Some would
attribute to decisions in eternity
the disorders of time.

Fire and gravel. Anything
might happen.

On an old chart of the New
World, off
the coast by Newport or,
perhaps, Japan, a bearded
Elemental gazes at the great
shell in his hands and

considers—like Wagner in
Würzburg—the fearful sounds he
will make but has
not yet made.

By the turn of thought in which
cause and effect
are rules in a geometry, our
progress falls against the
brightness of the day or
darkness of the night
sky.

Raised tones continue upward and
lowered tones drift down—part
of an attempt, merely,
to extend movement towards
the boundless and
"reconcile us to
life in general."

This pistol, like
any other, will
shoot only
into the future.

It's not troubling to me to
think the world to its
end, but I'm
deeply disturbed at
the edge of a map.

IN PASSING

Expression may be effected
without a slightest movement of any
facial muscle. A thought may be
forced out through the hands, for
example. See how nervous, then, these
fingers are.

Dangers I have not faced—dangers
of depth—are reflected on high,
warnings against too facile flight.
See, on this middle ground, whole
fleets of unlaunched craft, decaying.

Or the word 'passage' in the phrase *the
passage of time*—philosophers
debate its meaningfulness. For some,
there is only time, no passage. And
for others, of course, no time either.

See how the unseen sun, behind
that solid grey sky, obscures
the decline of the afternoon.

At birth whole
areas of the globe are
still uncommitted.
Something I just
picked up along
the way. My inertia,
well, my
inertia—I can
blame it on the constellations, can't I?
The pity is, in
'middle' life, I'm getting clumsy, mis-
calculating, now,
distances between my physical
influence and
various things, some of them
breakable. And I used to
slip by so carefully, skirting
an ambush of objects poised to fall, the
planet that presided
at my birth having been
in, oh, fastidious conjunction, but now—
this on high authority—losing
its grip, wandering (taking myself
as point of reference), and from now on
whatever controls there
are for my headlong
career must proceed directly
from the stars of the microcosm.

THE RUINS OF PROVIDENCE

Two oaks—in the afternoon, if
the sun is shining—cast their
shadows across Elmgrove
Avenue. Whether or not there was ever

a grove, the elms are gone.
Gone, too, in Kansas, though I
remember them luxuriant. The electric
company has hacked away

at the maple in front of my
house—chopping an airway
for their power—and it will
blaze yellow and red again this fall, but

I think it is dying. The sycamore in
back, still, sheds its bark
and shines. At least I will not
die in Kansas. Around the corner,

there are two gingko trees, fifteen
feet or so from each other—of different
sex, I suppose. It's hard to know
what to predict or even to prefer

for this terrain: oak forest like
primeval Europe, or endless gingko
grove. I love these wooden houses that
the rich built, and we live in.

Here, and in Saint Petersburg, one
dreams of being run over by
horses in the street. Saint
Petersburg, Russia, that is, at the
turn of the century. Since the Revolution
they are more and more (horses, I
mean) a thing of the past—or of
westerns. Which brings me
to Italy, where a torrent of traffic
rushes, honking, over
the Roman Empire. But here,
and through a desert, anytime, the Nile
flows like a dream.

from *SHIPWRECK IN HAVEN*

SIXTH TRANSCENDENTAL STUDY

Behind and above, I saw then everything
that was happening on earth and can
describe the hum of clouds. Why

are you screaming? East of the sycamore
is the other world. Look: the same
road, lisp and rustle. At length you

may come to no decision, straight
as a die. Ample time for
dancing between acts. I am relieved

the sycamore is healthy—at my
death I will go to it. Not
into it, but someday, if sufficiently

sensitive, you may
spot me, in the guise of child or
dwarf perhaps, leaning against the trunk like

a fallen branch. We are talking with
rhyme and reason, an art of
shading, smooth gradation

of loud and soft, velocity
distributed. Self-love, seeking
an object, splits

us in two. Nothing is
hidden from us, hour by
hour, with absolute certainty of its

occurrence. If I do
show up (perhaps as
dwarf or child) it will be to

the west—or south of the tree, *facing*
west. Children still of tender age are
taken into the forest and none of them

dare go home again, more and more
unfit for work, spending precious
time and learning nothing,

cantabile. You behold the wind coming
up the street. I doubt the easiness of
any access. Witness the horrors

of original scenery. First a
river. Then
a hill. What do you

bring that is good? The dead
pick these flowers and place them behind
their eyes and drink this water and have

no more desire. Good country near
the church. Twelve coffins
filled with shavings and in each

the little death pillow. The air is at
rest, belting around. Nothing
left for us to think about. Everything

proclaims the same language, not
the same thought. French windows, open
wide, flood the room with

regular patterns, like a military
parade. A large hall to
contain them. Pleasure at

every step. Soldiers swaying in the
breeze, their abundance and their
freedom. Counterblow to

night. I must devour you—skin,
hair and all. We must provide
for winter. Now let us examine

the dwellings of the kingdom
of heaven. What happens to
the severed parts? I hurl an axe

into the storm. Love potion: blood
dripping from the finger from one
year into the next. Hence my dread

of day's endless chain. When darkness
overtakes us, we will find no
shelter. I do not mind being

coachman on the box, but
drag you myself I
will not. Death is something

that occurs to a sleeper. Hair parted and
gathered in a Psyche knot back
of your head. Death

can strike the eye. Oh for me I
have other plans. Reason intervenes
to order impulse. Still, it

can appear—death—as
a solution, which of course
it is. Alone with your treasures,

hardly a budge to the little
ravine. Wild animals. Cry yourself
sleepy. I used to go to all

vampire films. Hope sprang
eternal. Lovers drink each
other's blood. First a river, then

a hill. A new vein opens. I
have admitted too many entities. Time
to razor down. I understand

how one might prefer to walk
bent over, eyes
to the pavement. We hear

horses neigh, soldiery laugh. Laid
waste, the farmers' fields. The cattle
killed. Men, women, slaughtered. Kings:

those that sleep. The king wears
a dragon mask. The king's soul
is lost and the king's soul is

found again. Dearest to each animal
its own constitution. Endless
causation. The king is not

what he seems to be. Death, disease,
weakness, being out of condition,
ugliness, and the like. If I

stir in my sleep, it is because the
point of a weapon has
touched us. It was my own

regard that quickened death, my
interest that made it personal.
Stories told by the fire at night making

creepy flesh, pneumatic
power, *cantabile*. You inspect
each one, lift it, put your

nose to it. Snow spreads a white
sheet over the grave. Will you
come? Verbatim. While wishing

still fulfills. Keep your eye
out for me, in the vicinity of
that tree. I will be

near it. Perhaps, in spring, as a child
reaching for the center. Look at the sycamore:
tall, healthy, flashing its regalia.